how to build a wax figure

Isabella Waldron

methuen | drama

LONDON • NEW YORK • OXFORD • NEW DELHI • SYDNEY

METHUEN DRAMA
Bloomsbury Publishing Plc
50 Bedford Square, London, WC1B 3DP, UK
1385 Broadway, New York, NY 10018, USA
29 Earlsfort Terrace, Dublin 2, Ireland

BLOOMSBURY, METHUEN DRAMA and the Methuen
Drama logo are trademarks of Bloomsbury Publishing Plc

First published in Great Britain 2022

Cover design: Kim Koch

Cover image © Nell Bailey

A catalogue record for this book is available from the British Library.

A catalog record for this book is available from the Library of Congress.

ISBN: PB: 978-1-3503-5175-2
ePDF: 978-1-3503-5176-9
eBook: 978-1-3503-5177-6

Series: Modern Plays

Typeset by Mark Heslington Ltd, Scarborough, North Yorkshire
Printed and bound in Great Britain

To find out more about our authors and books visit
www.bloomsbury.com and sign up for our newsletters.

how to build a wax figure

how to build a wax figure was first previewed at the Pleasance in February 2022, presented by November Theatre, with the following cast and creative team. *It was subsequently performed at Assembly, Edinburgh Fringe in August 2022 with a different cast.*

Bea	Lilit Lesser/Annabel Baldwin
Margot	Letty Thomas
Dana	Alice Franziska
Writer	Isabella Waldron
Director	Nell Bailey
Producer	Sarah Jordan-Verghese (Originating)
	Sophie Kilgannon (Assistant)
	Emma Ruse (Associate)
Designer	Ellie Roser

Letty Thomas (Margot) is an actor from London, whose work has crossed theatre and screen. Theatre credits include: *Scenes with Girls*, *Maryland* and *Living Newspaper* (Royal Court); *Square Rounds* (Finborough); *The Divide* (Old Vic); *Mary Stuart* (Almeida); *Men* (Arcola).

Film and television credits include: *Emma* (Working Title); *Damage* (Netflix); *The Crown* (Netflix); *Bridgerton* (Netflix); *Soulmates* (AMC); *Queens of Mystery* (ITV); *Doc Martin* (ITV); *Uneatable* (NFTS).

Annabel Baldwin (Bea) is an actor from London, who trained at ArtsEd.

Theatre credits include: *Pride and Prejudice Sort Of* (Criterion Theatre); *Harry Potter and the Cursed Child* (Palace Theatre); *Antigone* (New Diorama); *The Wolves* (Stratford East); *Wild Swimming* (Bristol Old Vic/Pleasance); *Scripted* (Sheffield Crucible); *Dear Elizabeth* (The Gate).

TV credits include: *Doctors*, *I Hate Suzie*, *The Great*, *The Jewish Enquirer*.

Voice credits include: *Persuasion* (Audible Original), *Our Wives Under the Sea* (Audiobook).

Annabel is currently writing and developing work of their own while continuing to workshop with various theatre companies and last year, completed an MA in Radio Production.

Alice Franziska (Dana) is signed with Middleweek Newton Talent Management. Her professional credits include *Motherland*, *The Burning Tower*, and the upcoming third season of *War of the Worlds*. While training with the 2019–2020 National Youth Theatre REP Company she performed as Estella in *Great Expectations*, Hippolyta and Cobweb in *A Midsummer Night's Dream* at the Criterion Theatre, and Sonya Serebryakov in extracts from *Uncle Vanya*. She is an original cast member of *how to build a wax figure*, and absolutely thrilled be a part of this complex, queer, unique coming of age story.

Nell Bailey (director) is a director whose practice is rooted in New Writing, Queer work, and community engagement. Having trained as an actor at RADA and Columbia University (USA), she transitioned into directing after founding November Theatre in 2019. Alongside NT, she has worked with Theatre Deli, the National Youth Theatre, The Silver Lining Co., and Harpy Productions. She has a background in film/TV script development in the UK and US with Killer Films, Braven Films and Early Day Films.

Ellie Roser (designer) is a Bristolian artist and performance designer now working in London. She has made work at The Bristol Old Vic, with The National Youth Theatre and as part of Brighton and Camden Fringe. With a background in devised performance and fine art, Ellie takes a multidisciplinary approach to her practice and she is interested in work grounded in community, sustainability and collaboration.

Isabella Waldron (writer) is an Oregon-born, London-based playwright with a passion for intergenerational, queer and women-led stories. Her play *Jawbone* was selected as a semi-finalist for the Bay Area Playwrights' Foundation 2022, the O'Neill National Playwrights Conference 2021, and is now being turned into an animated feature. *Things I Never Told the Stars* was selected as a semi-finalist for Bay Area Playwrights Foundation 2021. Her writing has also been featured with Frumpish Theatre at the Golden Goose, Silver Lining Co., 24 Hour Plays, Theatre NOVA, Our Digital Stories, The WorkShop Theatre, the Portland Actors' Conservatory, and as a San Francisco Chronicle Critic's Choice.

Sarah Jordan Verghese (producer) is a South Asian producer creating community-focused productions which aims to effect positive change to our society. She is excited by work that is culturally and political relevant, engages new audiences and is widely accessible. She is currently the producer at Nouveau Riche, creative producer at GymJam Theatre and assistant producer at Zoo Co. Her past projects include *I'm just a little bit OCD*, London Tour 2022; *Fester*, Camden Fringe Festival 2021 and *Every Sinner has a Future*, Kensington and Chelsea Festival and Golden Goose 2021.

Sophie Kilgannon (producer) is a producer with a passion and focus on feminist and women-led work. Sophie is excited by work that tackles contemporary issues and does not shy away from radical texts, aiming to create work that is accessible and engaging. Sophie is currently the producer for Drag collective 'Haus of Bollix' and has recently produced their show *Definitely Maybe Actually Nevermind* at The Space. She is also marketing assistant for Chain Reaction Theatre Company and producer of Paprichoo's *La Voisin*. Past works include *Little Fox's Christmas Adventure*, 2021; *La Voisin London Horror Fest*, 2021 and *Rewritten*, 2021.

Emma Ruse (producer) is a Scotland-based independent producer and co-founder of Framework Theatre Company, an organisation dedicated to delivering high-quality support to emerging theatre makers. She has a background in funding and policy, from her work as a member of the National Youth Arts Advisory Group for Scotland and the Year of Young People in 2018. She is also currently a committee member at Theatre Directors Scotland, and has recently worked with Perth Theatre and Vanishing Point.

November Theatre is a bold, transatlantic, new writing theatre company. Sprung from the vibrant theatre communities of NYC, November Theatre puts international writers in conversation with foreign environments. The company explores vital stories of love, friendship, and place in the world. As a supportive, development-led company, we work with writers from early ideas to fully realised productions, championing emerging artists and queer creators to tell excting new stories. Since their conception in the fall of 2019, November Theatre has staged a sold out production of Miriam Battye's *Pancake Day* at The Tank NYC, a workshop of Andy Jo's *Hananim*, and an online digital series hosted during COVID-19. Their first UK show, *how to build a wax figure* by Isabella Waldron, is set to premiere at Edinburgh Fringe festival in August 2022.

Founded by Nell Bailey and Britt Berke, NT is based in NYC and London.

Acknowledgements/Thank you

With thanks to

Nell for reading my mind, telling me when to stop overhauling, and championing this play with heart and tenacity. You are a gift. Lilit, Beth, Letty, Annabel, Alice and all the other actors that have brought questions and thoughts and general brilliance.

Arts Council England, London Performance Studios and New Diorama Theatre for providing the scaffolding we needed to make this play. The Georgias at Frumpish Theatre and the Golden Goose for giving us our first stage. Bill at the Gordon Museum of Pathology for letting me come and look at gruesome wax figures until I felt ill. Jodie, Kim, Dave, Sam, Bel, Sarah, Sophie, and Emma for your incredible support of this story.

Eloise, Corbin and Rachel for always showing up. Josh for making theatre warm and wild and reading everything I send. Phoebe, Siobhan, and Issy for your love and our home. And my mum, Luisa Sermol, for making me run lines with her in the Volvo so many times that I started writing my own.

In the text

On casting: Bea can be cast with a non-binary actor, and if that is the case, please feel free to change pronouns for older Bea according to what the team feels fits. These suggested changes were developed in conversation with previous actors and are well within the world of the script.

On pace: end punctuation and verse breaks are intentional and should mark changes in pace throughout. / marks an interruption.

On changes: transitions should be done by actors and can and should be seen by the audience.

Please note that the published script went to press before the end of rehearsals, so may be slightly different to what was performed on stage.

how to build a wax figure

For someone not to notice the reality of it is my favourite part
– Christie Erickson, Ocularist

Cast

Bea, *ages 17–25 throughout the play. Woman. The Ocularist.*
Margot, *ages 32–39 throughout the play. Woman. The Sculptor.*
Dana, *late 20s/early 30s. Woman. The Facilitator.*

Setting

Wellcome Collection storage room; Margot's sculpting studio

Set should be sparse; only a few markings to differentiate location/time

The wax models are up to production's interpretation. Could be full wax models, a mannequin, wire shaped loosely into a human-esque form and covered in cloth, etc.

scene one

Storage room somewhere in the abyss of the Wellcome Collection that may or may not exist. An old and noisy slide projector, conference tables stacked, lamps, odd scientific exhibition rejects here and there. Projected videos of a magnified human eyeball and a prosthetic eye being pushed into a mould alternate back and forth. **Bea** *is alone, clutching a box of prosthetic eyeballs and practicing her lecture.*

Bea A dart, car door, hockey puck, hockey stick, paintball, a tomato stake in a garden
What do these things have in common?
All cause for a lost eye
And then there's the heavier ones
Cancer, diabetes

Chorus of text noises chime from everywhere across the room. Ceiling, depths of the floors, audience, etc.

Projection of one text. **Margot**'s *voice comes amplified from offstage.*

Margot Hey – me.
Out of the blue, I know, but do you fancy a drink sometime soon? Catch up? Thinking of you
Hope all is well x

The room shakes.

Dana *enters with a cake box, one plate, one fork.*

Dana Hello? Is someone in here?

Bea *spills the box of eyeballs all over the stage. They go everywhere. Huge colossal mess.*

Bea FUCK
Sorry

Dana What are you doing in here?

Bea Great. Perfect.
I'm supposed to be presenting – lecturing –
upstairs and I don't know what's happening

but I feel like it's a hundred degrees and I'm –
Can you see my sweat through this shirt?

Dana   No!
Well, barely

Bea   I put a pad in my armpit – I'm not even kidding – I
really – there's a pad in my armpit right now because I sweat
so much when I'm nervous I'm not being funny I sweat
through a *coat* once in school and – Sorry, did you just hear a
phone buzz?

Dana   Are you alright?

Dana *sets down the cake box.*

Bea   No

Dana   Oh
Well
Here, here, let me help you

Dana *silently continues picking up the eyeballs. She is careful. She
polishes each one on her blouse before putting it back in the box.* **Bea**
watches her.

Dana   Assuming your lecture's got something to do with
eyes then?

Bea   Ocularistry
I can't go in
I feel ill

Dana   We can hide out here for a bit if you like
It's a good place for that

Bea   I'm late already

Dana   Just while we clean up

Bea *kneels down to help* **Dana** *collect eyeballs.*

Bea   I don't know why they've hired me
They've made a horrible mistake

Dana   I wouldn't tell them that

Bea   I have a joke in my notes:
This is not eye health nor is it witchcraft
It's a bit in the middle
Some say art, some say science
What say you?
That's not even a joke is it?
She'd be great at this
Fuck
She'd probably sculpt the audience or something
They'd laugh at her jokes and she's not even funny

Dana   She?

Bea   Sorry
A friend or um
a mentor I guess

Dana   Where's everyone always getting these mentors from?

Bea   What do you do?

Dana   She was an ocularist?

Dana *hides her badge away.*

Bea   Um
Wax sculptor, actually
Anatomical and dermatological models
for doctors and medical schools and all that
Hideous diseases in three-dimensional form
I made the eyes for her
Sorry, this is not – this day is not supposed to be about
Margot

Margot *enters from behind the projection screen or somewhere similarly nonsensical.*

Margot   Why can't it be about me?
Just a little bit?

Dana   She taught you how to make eyes

Bea   Well, first she taught me how to make people

Dana   Naturally

Margot *approaches* **Bea**.

Bea   You've got to watch videos, photos, see how your
subject slopes, how they limp, how their left eye slides
outward just so and then you start building
Some people – Madame Tussauds – will use a plaster mould
and coat it in a thin hot wax but Margot only used a soft
prototyping wax called 1704 white
You can get it from British Wax in Redhill
She'd start with wire and build up from there, moulding it in
broad strokes
and then smaller and more refined like a surgeon, you know,
drilling down and down until it's just

Dana *fades*.

Bea   Human

Margot *and* **Bea** *transform the stage into* **Margot**'s *temperature-controlled wax studio, filled with gruesome anatomical wax models.*

Bea   I started going over to her studio when I was
seventeen
She moved in next door
There weren't a lot of interesting people in town
and she was very
Interesting

Bea *is holding a wax head.* **Margot** *is busy somewhere else.*

Margot   Bea, if you're going to stick around, could you
make yourself useful?

Bea   Why has this head got a horn on it?
Can humans have horns?

Margot   Don't touch anything!

Bea   I'm not!

Bea *puts the head down.*

Margot *re-enters.*

Bea   Our last neighbour had a tea cosy collection
and you've got a head with a horn on it

Margot   Cutaneous horn
Just a skin lesion, essentially

Bea   Cool
I like how it smells in here too

Margot   Does it smell?

Bea   Yeah, like stewed apples and
stamps

Margot   Wax, please

Bea *hands* **Margot** *wax.*

scene two

Shift back to the Wellcome Collection.

Bea   She was her work
She didn't spend time with anyone else as far as I could tell
My mother hated her
And the figures
I mean, you can imagine:

Mother (*V/O*)   You can't be friends with a thirty-two-year-
old woman

Bea   Why not?

Mother (*V/O*)   Because you're fifteen

Bea   I'm seventeen, Mum

Mother (*V/O*)   If she were a man, I would be arrested for
child neglect

Bea   She's not

Mother (*V/O*)   Well, she's strange
And besides her age, it's all those statues/

Bea   Figures/

Mother (*V/O*)   They're terrifying and they're going to give you nightmares

Bea   Please can I be excused now

Mother (*V/O*)   Finish your beans

Bea *chomps 'em down.*

Bea   Please can I be excused now

Mother (*V/O*)   Does she smoke?

Margot *starts smoking from her chair.*

Bea   No

Shift to studio.

Margot *is smoking out the window of the studio.*

Margot   You want some? You smoke right?

Bea   Yes

Bea *takes the cigarette, coughs violently.*

Margot *smiles.*

Margot   Here, try this

Smell my wrist

She extends her wrist to **Bea***'s nose.*

Bea *inhales.*

Margot   Now do that again but with the cigarette

She holds the cig for **Bea***, lights it.*

Margot   Breathe in

Bea *inhales deep.*

Margot   Good

Everything on stage begins to dance a little bit; subtly, softly.

Margot *sculpts.*

Bea   How did you get so good at it

Margot   Smoking or sculpting?

Bea   Sculpting

Margot   Am I?

Bea   Good at it?

Margot   Mm

Bea   Obviously, Margot

Margot   Well, I think about it all the time
and I do it all the time
and I love it all the time
Mm – not all the time
but I love it

Bea   You're so cool

Margot *laughs.*

Margot   Likewise, little Bea
You could be great at it, you know
Sculpting

Bea   My mother says she'll murder me if I become an artist

Margot   Good woman.

Margot *adds clay to a model she is shaping.*

It is painstaking work
It's painful work
Look at this
See this man?

Margot *pulls up a photo that is amplified on the projector.*

Bea   What is that?

Margot   Tertiary syphilis
Horrible
Not what you want

Bea   Don't you ever get sad sculpting all these sick people

Margot   No, I think it's nice that someone's spending this much time on them
And it's art, after all
I'm not a doctor

Bea   You could be

Margot   I'd make much more money
But then look at this

She pulls up a figure of an Anatomical Venus.

I mean it's just delicious, isn't it
She's got real human hair
She's got pearls
She's got fucking satin cushions
That's past medicine

Bea   She's very . . .

Margot   Sexy? It's the Susini models.

Bea   Or like those old saints
My mum's got tons of photos of those old saints and they pull the same face
Of um what's it
Not excited –
Ecstatic
Like
Like belonging to another world
It looks like she's being abducted by aliens
But like spiritual aliens maybe
Like god I guess
I don't know
That's wrong, isn't it

Margot   No
I just haven't seen them like that before
They are stunning models. Sometime we'll go. Field trip to
Florence. You'll love them.
For now, the mouldings.
You have to have everything absolutely perfect
Here, the eye socket, see?
You can feel your own – like this

Margot *demonstrates*.

so you can see where the eyeball will sit

Bea   Who does the eyes?

Margot   I will on occasion
Usually I just order them though
They're a bugger to get perfect

Bea   Can I try?

Margot   The eyes?
Bit out of my wheelhouse, but sure
I've got the equipment

Bea   I have a steady hand

Margot   Alright.
Come here

Margot *lingers behind* **Bea**.

scene three

Dana *reappears behind* **Bea**'s *other shoulder*.

Dana   I'm just gonna eat my lunch. Go on, please go on,
but just –
I've got low blood sugar

Bea   Oh, yes please
Sorry I'm rambling –

Dana   No, no, please

Dana *whips out a birthday cake.*

Bea   Sorry, is that a cake?

Dana   It's um

It's my birthday, yeah

Bea (*sung*)   Happy / Birthday

Dana   NO
Please no
It's depressing

Gets a candle and puts it on top.

I just like the cake bit
It's vanilla
I made it

Bea   You made your own birthday cake?

Dana   Go on then
She showed you how to make a person and then she showed
you how to make eyes

Laughs.

Not like that

Bea   Well . . .

Dana   Oh?

Bea   No, I mean,
Not then

Bea *and* **Margot** *are working.* **Bea** *wordlessly hands* **Margot**
things she needs. Music in the background. **Margot** *begins dancing
as she sculpts.* **Bea** *watches, standing still and awkward.*

Margot   C'mon you! Boogie!

Bea *shakes her head.*

Bea   I hate dancing

Margot   Oh nobody hates dancing

Bea   I imagine plenty of people hate dancing

Margot   You'll look silly
So what who cares it's just me

Bea *hesitates for a long time as* **Margot***'s moves get progressively larger.*

Eventually she starts nodding her head to the beat a bit.

Margot   YES BEA! That's it! Go on!

Bea *gets a bit more into it, starts using her legs or arms albeit awkwardly – a bit like a duckling learning to swim.* **Margot** *is laughing, but with her. She mirrors* **Bea***.* **Bea** *gets sillier.*

Margot   That's BEAUTIFUL

The dance builds. They're dancing and dancing big and huge and the song ends and they are breathless.

Margot   Alright, back to work

Margot *turns back to the bench.* **Bea** *turns back to* **Dana***.*

Bea   Not right then

Dana *licks the frosting.*

Bea   But, you're right, I was the eyes and she was the body
I mean that sounds poetic but really that's how it worked
I did turn out to have a steady hand and it helped and I
loved it
The spinning orb, painting the pupil
and then matching the iris
The thin red thread to mark the veins
And I liked that she would watch me work
I spent every afternoon in the studio with her

Dana   Making eyes

scene four

The studio. **Bea** *is 18.*

Margot   Are you staying for dinner then?

Bea   Can't

Margot   What big plans have you got then

Bea   My mum wants me home
because tomorrow

Margot   Because tomorrow what

Bea   Because tomorrow I leave?

Margot *sets down the sculpting clay.*

Margot   No you don't

Bea   Yes I do

Margot   I thought that was months away

Bea   I told you before
It's only for –

Margot   What am I going to do without you?

Bea   It's only for / a while

Margot   No, no, sweet Bea
I'm being a bat
Of course you will go. Of course you will.
God, I forget sometimes
You're so young, aren't you?

Bea   I don't like when you say that
I'm eighteen

Margot *snort-laughs.*

Margot   You're going to study amazing art / and become

Bea   I'm not going for art

Margot   What do you mean you're not going for art?

Bea   I'm going for medicine.
To be a doctor.
Or a nurse.
I don't know.

Margot (*disgust*)   Medicine?

Bea *shrugs in acknowledgment.*

Margot   What will they do with you in medicine?
You're an artist, Bea

Bea   I don't know
I thought it'd be more helpful

Margot *continues working in silence for a minute.*

Bea   Are you mad at me?

Margot   No.
No!
Why would I be mad?

Bea   I don't know
You seem mad

Margot   You're interpreting

Beat.

I'm not mad, Bea

Bea   Okay.

Because you really can't be mad at me for leaving when you haven't even asked me to stay or anything

Margot   Asked you to stay?

Bea   Yeah

Margot   You don't belong to me

Bea   No?

Pregnant pause.

Margot   Well. I need to finish this up
Probably best to just head home and finish your packing
Don't want to keep you.

Bea   Okay.

Margot   I'd have picked something up, you know, if I'd known

Bea *gathers her things.*

Bea   Uh
I guess I'll just see you when I'm home then?

Margot   I mean, text me, right?
Or call sometime
Or don't! Live your life and I'll see you when you're all grown up and doctor-y
Or nurse-y.
University is a special time.

Bea *lingers, waiting for something more.*

Margot *smiles overenthusiastically.*

Margot   C'mon, shoo! Shouldn't you be saying bye to your friends instead of me?

Bea   I don't have friends besides you

Margot   Don't be dramatic
I'm just your funny old neighbour

Bea *moves close to* **Margot**.

They stay centimetres away from each other in pre-kiss for a weirdly long time.

Hushed.

Margot   You should go, Bea
Little Bea.

Stings. **Bea** *silently picks up her things and closes the door.* **Margot** *picks up the clay to work again but can't.*

scene five

A phone chimes, bringing us sharply back to the Wellcome Collection.

Bea *looks around for her phone a bit frantically.* **Dana** *sets down the cake, checks her phone.*

Dana   Oh, it's me

Bea   Oh.

Chorus of text sounds gets louder.

You're popular

Dana   People crawling out of the woodwork to congratulate me on aging as if I had any say in it

Chorus of text sounds gets increasingly louder.

I should take this
Would you watch the cake?
I'll be right back

Dana *exits. Loud clicking of the projector. Sudden shift.* **Bea**'s *in university. A series of text exchanges are displayed on the projector. Each slide shows a new text. The sound of a slide projector flicking through. The bold, italicised text marks the text messages themselves, fully-formed. The un-bolded, un-italicised text marks the drafting.*

Margot   *Hey sweet Bea*
Long time no chat
How's uni

Bea   I wait six hours to respond

Text sending sound.

hey! I know! things have been soooo busy here

Margot   *Good busy?*

Bea   *good busy*

Margot   *Lots of new friends?*

Bea   *some :-)*

Margot . . ./

Bea   *how are you?*

Margot   *Good.*

***Pretty good**

Bea   *working on?*

Margot   *Gout.*

. . .

Bea   Typing . . .

Margot   *Miss your eyes*

Bea *sits with that one for a moment, staring at the text on the projector with pleasure.*

Bea   *miss you*

The projection shifts. Date: a few weeks later.

It keeps going.
Every day.
I keep waiting for her to get bored of me and stop responding but she never does
And now she's using lowercase too and that feels significant because I know she's all attention to detail and so in switching to lowercase she's taking on my language
She's trying to be younger which in some way means she's trying to impress me or that at least she feels self-conscious which feels like a win

Rapid-fire texts on the projector, one after the other. A flurry of text chimes.

I text her whenever I like then because I feel like it isn't going to just end anymore, like whatever I say or however quickly I respond we are in a different kind of game with it now
saw your doppelganger in a bar last night

Margot   *did you buy her a drink*

Bea   *she wouldn't go for me*

Margot   *wouldn't be so sure*

Bea   *2 old*

Margot   *what are you implying . . .*

Bea   *hehe*
God. Ew.
Was that too far that might have been too far for –
Ooh – Typing . . .

Margot   *when do you come home?*

Bea   Fuck.
That was it
There.
Then.
I took the train home that weekend.

Margot *takes* **Bea***'s hand and pulls her to the studio. She sets it up.*

scene six

Margot *and* **Bea** *are sitting with two glasses of wine in the studio. Their conversation is weirdly formal.*

Margot   Uh how was the trip, the train?

Bea   Good.
Pretty views.

Margot   Nice
You're happy there then?

Bea   Yeah

Margot   Little Bea in the big city
You are so wonderful, you know that?

Bea   Uch

Margot   Seriously! I wish I was half as put together as you
when I was your age

Bea   Don't do that

Margot   Do what?

Bea   When I was your age   ·
You're acting like an estranged relative

Margot   Sorry. I just meant/

Bea   Can we work?

Margot   You want to work? Now?

Bea   What we always do isn't it
And I've missed it
Painting for you

Margot   Sure.
Okay.

Goes to wax sculpture.

I have to do the pores for this sad woman

Bea   Where's the orange

Margot   I'm using limes now
Ten times better

Bea *gets a lime.*

Margot   Here, look

Bea *pulls stool over to* **Margot**.

Margot *rolls the lime across the figure's skin gently to make pores.*

They are close.

Margot   You see that?
The light bounces so much better
In the morning, you'll see
Here, you go –

Margot *hands* **Bea** *the lime*.

Bea *kisses* **Margot**.

Margot *kisses* **Bea**.

They stop. Lime tight in **Bea**'s *hand*.

Margot   Is this . . .

Have we crossed a line?

Bea   Yes, but I think that was a while ago

Margot   Okay
Do you feel . . .
How do you feel?

Bea   Um.
Good
Bright
Do you . . . what about you?

Margot   Yeah, yeah, I mean
Good.
Bright.
Also.

Bea   Will you kiss me again?

Margot *kisses* **Bea** *again*.

Bea   Wait – it's / just

Margot   Is it too weird does it feel icky / or

Bea   No, it's her.

Gestures to wax sculpture.

I don't really . . . I don't really want them watching me
watching us

Margot   We can go upstairs?

Bea   I've never been up there

Margot   Yes, you have

Bea   No I haven't

Margot   Hmm
Feels like you have

scene seven

Wellcome Collection. **Dana** *re-enters.*

Dana   If one more person calls me singing, I'm going to lose it
Why do people think that's okay? And if you're going to do it, at least try to be on key, do you know what I mean?
Are you alright?

Bea   Me?

Dana   You

Bea   Yeah, just
I should find whoever hired me
Explain I can't do the lecture

Dana   No, don't do that

Bea   You're not a very good influence

Dana *sits on the floor, puts a candle in cake.*

Dana   It's my birthday
And you haven't even really gotten to the eyes yet

Bea   Okay, okay, the eyes
I think I'm quite good at detail actually
Which you need, to be / any good as –

Margot   BEA

Bea   As an / ocularist

Margot   BEA, I NEED YOU

Back to the studio. **Margot** *is sculpting.*

Bea *comes downstairs carrying 'The Secret'.*

Bea   I can't believe you own The Secret

Margot   Where did you find that

Bea   It was just sitting here!
Isn't this a little dated now?

Margot   I haven't read it

Bea   It's bookmarked on like every five pages

Margot   Give me that

Margot *struggles for the book.*

Bea *giggles and keeps it out of reach.*

Bea (*reading as she skirts* **Margot**)   'You are the masterpiece
of your own life.
You are the Michelangelo /
of your own life.'

Margot   GIVE / IT

Bea   'The David you are sculpturing
is you'

Margot *swats the book away from* **Bea**.

Margot   Come here, I want to sculpt you

Bea   Me? Really?

Margot   Yes, you
Just sit across from me. C'mon.

Bea *sits.* **Margot** *studies her.*

Bea   Do you believe that stuff?

Margot   I want to

Bea   Why

Margot   Because then I know that the only reason I'm not rich and fabulous is just because I haven't told the universe to make me that yet

Bea   No, really.

Margot   Hand, please

Margot *takes* **Bea**'s *hand and studies it for a moment.*

Margot   I don't know, I suppose
It'd be nice to know that
It's in my control
So the good things, that's me
and then the bad things, the really horrible things, that's me
I must have attracted that too
Just makes things simpler, doesn't it

Bea   You don't attract horrible things

Margot   Stay still

Bea   You didn't attract the shit stuff, Margot
That stuff just happens on its own

Margot   Let's not talk about this anymore please

Beat.

Bea   If I started melting one day would you clean me up

Margot   What are you on about, you loon

Bea   I woke up this morning with you there
and I felt
fluid
Like I might melt into a puddle at any minute
In a good way
Like it's in my stomach and exciting
But also like I might make a mess
Does that make sense?
Like when I'm in the real world
When my friends at uni are texting about a night out or
something

I feel solid
And feeling solid doesn't feel that good anymore
Feeling solid is boring and boxy and scratchy in my skin
And being with you is all liquid and gooey and there's just
no time at all
You know?

Margot   I like being liquid with you

Bea   But you're the only one I have, really, who will clean
me up
If I
Melt *too* much
And lose my shape
But you would
Clean me up
Right?
You'd tell me when it's too much?

Margot   I'll keep you at a nice room temperature, sweet
Bea

Bea   Send me a frequency

Margot   Be still

Bea   C'mon

Margot   Fine.

Beat.

There I sent one. Did you get it?

Bea   Yeah I got it

Caught somewhere between memory and present.

I stayed longer than I should have
Probably

scene eight

Middle of the night. **Bea** *at the workbench, making eyes, alone at first. Spinning the threads, trance like.* **Margot** *gets up, watches in the background for a minute. She disappears for a moment, returns with a glass of water. Sets it beside* **Bea** . . .

Bea   Did I wake you?

Margot *shakes her head.*

Margot   Couldn't sleep anyway

Margot *kisses* **Bea**'s *head, sits nearby, pulls a blanket around her and smokes out the window.*

Bea *looks over; keeps spinning the threads.*

scene nine

Wellcome Collection comes back into existence around **Bea**.

Dana *lights the candle on her cake, blows it out almost immediately. The noise shifts* **Bea** *out of memory.* **Margot** *lingers behind.*

Dana   I wish for the same thing every year
I figure if I do it enough times with exactly the same wish
my odds of it actually working are statistically increased

Bea   Won't ask what you wished for then

Dana   Won't tell you

Bea   I'm telling *you* things

Dana   And I'm enjoying the company

Bea   Are you? I'm a bit of a disaster right now

Dana   Well, you know what they say about car crashes

Bea   Oh, great

Dana   I'm kidding. I don't find you disastrous.
Here let's get these cleaned up

Dana *picks up an eyeball. She inspects it.*

Dana   They look so real. I mean, it must be like having a thousand people watching you at your desk. Don't you get creeped out?

Bea   I mean, it's an illusion. Prosthetic eyes, wax figures, but
You have someone, you know?
At least somebody's there with you

Dana   Jesus, that's grim

Beat.

Could you make me purple ones?

Bea (*distracted*)   Purple?

Dana   Yeah, I always wanted purple eyes when I was little
I've got really boring eyes

Bea   Oh?

Dana   I mean, look

Dana *scoots closer to* **Bea.**

Bea   You've got massive pupils

Dana   Really? Is that weird?

Bea   Normal.
For cats.

Dana *laughs.*

Margot *comes close to* **Bea.**

Margot   You flirting now?

Bea (*back to* **Margot**)   That's not fair

Dana   What?

Bea (*back to* **Dana**)   Sorry. Not you.

Margot   Come on. Come home.

scene ten

The studio. **Bea** *is making an eyeball.* **Margot** *is sculpting.*

Bea   Anyway the programme's great
It's medicine adjacent so nothing I learned so far will be
wasted really
and it's only a turnpike away
so it's not like it would be hard to visit each other

Margot *is quiet.*

Bea   What are you thinking?
Do you think I shouldn't?
Margot?

Margot   Isn't it odd? Us? To your friends
Do they think I'm predatory?

Bea   No?

Margot   I find that hard to believe

Bea   They don't care
I love you

Beat.

Margot   Do you ever wonder why I haven't said I love you

Bea   Yes, you have

Margot   I haven't though
I don't know – I can't stop thinking about it
I think about it all the time
Why I can't
If it's the age or if it's just –
You're so sweet and good and smart and / beautiful
But I can't

Bea   You're thinking too much again

Margot (*softly*)   I have been
I don't think it's fixable, Bea

Once I feel a certain way, you know, it's just what it is
You know me

Beat.

Bea   So then it was just the brief period when I become old
enough for you not to get in trouble, young supple body and
all that, and then it was enough

Margot   We have different lives, Bea

Margot *continues sculpting.*

You'd leave me at some point anyway
I'm just pointing out the inevitable

Bea   I am not going to leave you, shut up

Margot   You're too young, Bea
I mean, even if that's not *all* of it
it's certainly some of it

Bea   Stop it! I told you not to do that

Margot   I'm being logical.
Bea, my life exists within this room.
It's just me and the figures
You don't want to get stuck here with me
Making glass eyeballs all your life

Bea   That is *all* I want

Margot   Oh God

Bea   What's so wrong with that?

Margot   You need to go live in the world.
Find what you love.
Who you love/
You know

Bea   *Who* I love
Ohmygod
You're such a narcissist
I can't even believe it!

It's actually hilarious how much you think about yourself
You know what, maybe you're right, maybe you did attract
all the bad stuff
Manifested your way right into a life fully alone. / Nice one.

Margot   I'm seeing someone

Bea   What?

Margot   An osteopath. In London.
He's a bit older
Than me, I mean

Bea   *He*

Margot *shrugs.*

Margot   I want a baby, Bea

Bea   What? You've never *ever* said that before

Margot   Well, I *might* want one
I'm at an age / where

Bea   You want a baby HAHAHAHA
Oh God
You with a baby
Can you imagine
How fucked up that baby will be?
HAHAHA

Margot   Well, you're just proving my point aren't you
Two people have to be on the same level of life to really
understand each other/

Bea   A baby won't fix you

Margot   / And we clearly do not understand each other

Bea   Are you gonna fuck its friends then when they turn
eighteen?

Beat.

Margot   Go home, Bea.

scene eleven

Bea *is lost for a moment, somewhere between the Wellcome Collection and* **Margot***'s studio. The projector gets caught on a slide, flickers.* **Bea** *looks around her. Nobody is there . . .*

scene twelve

Shift back to the Wellcome Collection.

Bea *is quiet for a moment.*

Dana   So I'll take that as a no to cake?
That's fine
I mean, I did make the fondant by hand
but no
That's fine

Bea *shakes the memory off, slowly. Like shedding a skin.*

Bea   Hi
You're here

Dana   Hello
I haven't left?

Bea   Sorry
I'm sorry for rambling
Um
You know
I don't even know your name?
That's horrible
What's your name?

Dana   Dana

Bea   Dana.

Wait . . . As in –

Dana   Yeah, I'm the one you've been emailing with. I'm um
I'm Wellcome Collection Dana

Bea   Why didn't you say something? I've just been – I
didn't know I knew you
We're like thirty minutes late – aren't you going to be fired?

Dana   I might be, but I'm in a self-destructive mood today
apparently
I'm sorry for not saying anything
I just – you started talking about the eyes and the wax and
the. . .
I wanted to hear
Not as Wellcome Collection Dana, you know?

Bea   But you are Wellcome Collection Dana

Dana   I mean, from nine-to-five yes
I'm sorry I didn't say anything
You were just so wound up

It's like hiccups maybe

Bea   What?

Dana   When you have hiccups and someone surprises you
and you forget about your hiccups because you're surprised?
You look less sweaty now. Less nervous, I mean

Bea   That's another illusion then

Dana   You were just being so open and I didn't want to
startle you

Bea   Okay, I'm not a fucking deer

Dana   Well, what did you think I was doing in the storage
room?

Bea   I don't know! Just eating cake!
I wouldn't have shared all that if I knew you had *hired* me

Dana   I don't hire
I just facilitate

Bea   Well, it was weird of you to not say anything and now
I'm more freaked out for this stupid lecture which I really

shouldn't be giving at all because I'm definitely not qualified
and definitely not inspiring

Dana   You don't have to be inspiring

Bea   Oh, great, thanks
I need a cigarette

Bea *rifles through her bag without luck.*

Do you have a cigarette
I was trying to quit

Dana   I don't smoke

Bea   Of course you don't

Dana   I've got the lighter?

Offers **Bea** *the lighter she used earlier for her birthday candle.*

Bea *takes the lighter and rushes out.*

scene thirteen

Shift to outside smoking area.

Bea *is by herself for a moment, holding the lighter.*

Then, **Margot** *appears.*

Bea   God can you
LEAVE
ME
ALONE
PLEASE

Margot   Bea?

Bea

Margot   Shouldn't you be lecturing

Bea   Margot?

Margot   Alright, maybe I *should* go for Botox
It's not been *that* long

Bea   Few years

Margot   Has it been?

Cig?

Bea   Fine

Margot *gives* **Bea** *a cigarette.*

Margot   I'm late
Sorry

Bea   What do you mean you're late

Margot   To your lecture
I was just going to pop in the back quietly
Listen
Sent that text earlier thought I might catch you after

Bea   How did you know I was doing this
Did my mum tell you / I was doing this

Margot   I recommended you

Bea   Fuckssake

Margot   They've got three of my figures
Smallpox, leprosy, bubonic plague
They asked if I knew anyone
Your mum said you were having a hard time

Bea   Well, she's mistaken
I'm doing incredibly well

Margot   Right/

Bea   And don't talk to her anyways

Margot   She's my neighbour

Bea   Well she's my mother

Margot   Are we doing this?

Bea   Sorry I'm just

Sighs.

Sorry.
It's Weird
To see you
Outside of my head

Margot   Right.

Bea   How's what's-his-name

Margot   Who?

Bea   Your osteopath

Margot   Oh. We're um . . . It didn't work out

Bea   Sorry

Margot   Oh, ages ago

Waves it off.

I guess I should / apologize

Bea   Please – just –
I don't want to do that
I don't want to do the whole I'm sorry and –
I don't want to do that with you

Margot   Fine, alright

Bea   Why'd you text me?

Margot   You like the eyes? Still?
Making the eyes?

Bea   I do. Yeah. I do.

Margot   I hope it wasn't . . .

Bea   What?

Margot   Because of me
I mean you could have been
I don't know
Making huge messy oil paintings

Acclaimed abstract artist
or a surgeon, you could have been this incredible surgeon
and I just hope that I didn't . . .
I don't know
That you could have had something bigger

Beat.

Bea   They're such a personal item
Eyes
And people are quite open
when replacing one
They tell me things I don't ask to know about, write me
emails after their appointments about what they've done
with their new eyes, and it makes the world bigger for me
This man came in at the end of the year with his wife and he
didn't have a lot going for him to be honest, but his eyes
were
Stunners, cerulean
but he tripped and hit the radiator and out it went
I know. Horrible.
I made him an eye. That's all
And then at the end of his cleaning a few months in, right
before they left, his wife popped back in, asked if I would
make an extra set so that when he dies she can keep his eyes.
Look at them before she goes to sleep
I mean she just told me that like it was nothing
Sat there blinking at me and I started crying
Because
Most things in the world are enormous
Have you ever thought about that?
Even an eyeball
is much more than an eyeball
Even an atom
is an enormous thought
Everything
Is
Huge
and

Impossible
And I want that

Margot   Bea I'm / sorry for minimizing

Bea   No, don't apologize
It's too obvious, Margot
It's too on the nail
and it –
It makes things
between us
seem
wrong

It wasn't all bad
I mean some of it was horribly bad
but a lot of it was

a lot of it was really
wonderfully
good

Margot   Hugely good

Bea   And I love what I do, okay?
Not because of you
but not *not* because of you either

Margot   Okay

So that drink/

Bea   I mean obviously I want to
but . . .

Margot   Right
Well, if you change your mind I'm staying in town / tonight
at the

Bea   Don't tell me because I'll go if you do, okay?

Beat.

Margot *smiles.*

Margot   You really shouldn't smoke
It'll ruin your lungs

Bea   You should go
I have to do my lecture
Haven't started out very well

Margot   Start from scratch

Bea   Be nice, wouldn't it

Margot   Yeah. Then . . .

Bea   Then . . .
I'll see you

Margot *nods.*

Margot   At home
Sometime
Sweet Bea

Margot *exits.*

Shift.

Bea *stubs out her cigarette.*

scene fourteen

Bea *enters the Wellcome Collection lecture room.* **Dana** *is gathering the last few eyeballs into their box. She has boxed up the rest of the cake.*

Dana (*handing cake to* **Dana**)   In case you change your mind

Bea   I'm sorry about earlier
About just talking at you like you weren't –
I think I might be just a really fucked up person
I don't know if I started out that way or ended up this way
but/

Dana *snort-laughs.*

Bea Sorry?

Dana Well, obviously you are

Bea Wow. Okay?

Dana I kissed my cousin

Bea What?

Dana I mean second cousin
but still

Bea I guess kids / do that

Dana Nope, we weren't that young
And it was more than once
And it was nice actually

Bea Why are you telling / me this

Dana Because you get here all sweaty and clumsy with
eyeballs and self-doubty and it's you being an artist and
Meanwhile I've got to plan the events and provide coffee
and create some sort of illusion that the world is actually
very orderly and together and professional which we both
know it's not
And your madness gets to be art and my madness gets
buried underneath an ongoing stream of Excel proficiency
and save-the-dates and birthday cake alone in this room
until I die. And actually, as I've sat here watching you
implode, I'm wondering how on earth is that fair?

Beat.

Bea That complicates Christmas
The cousin thing

Dana Oh, no, Christmas was quite good
Mistletoe and all that
No questions asked

Bea Can I buy you a drink?

Dana What?

Bea   I'd like to buy you a drink
For your birthday
I won't sing to you, I promise

Dana   Oh.
Yes
I'd like that
After your lecture
If you still want to. I can always say you had a family
emergency or / something, disappear through the exit route.

Bea   No, I want to do it

Dana   Good. I want to hear it.

Dana *collects herself, smooths out her clothing. Hands* **Bea** *the box of eyeballs.*

Dana   Have you ever done your own, by the way?

Bea   Eyes? No

Dana   You should
They're nice ones
You can kinda see you thinking through them
That sounded weird

Bea   No it doesn't
Thank you

Beat.

Dana   I uh
need to put out the complimentary snacks
They'll be foaming at the mouth by now

Bea   I'll meet you in there

Dana   Kay, Good
Cool
Great
Good

Dana *nods, laughs nervously, exits.*

Bea *begins packing up. She packs the box of eyeballs up, looks at her notes.*

Bea This is not eye health nor is it witchcraft
It's a bit in the middle
Some say art, some say science
I say –

The projection shutters off.

Darkness; something new; something unknown.

End play.

Methuen Drama Modern Plays

include

Bola Agbaje
Edward Albee
Ayad Akhtar
Jean Anouilh
John Arden
Peter Barnes
Sebastian Barry
Clare Barron
Alistair Beaton
Brendan Behan
Edward Bond
William Boyd
Bertolt Brecht
Howard Brenton
Amelia Bullmore
Anthony Burgess
Leo Butler
Jim Cartwright
Lolita Chakrabarti
Caryl Churchill
Lucinda Coxon
Tim Crouch
Shelagh Delaney
Ishy Din
Claire Dowie
David Edgar
David Eldridge
Dario Fo
Michael Frayn
John Godber
James Graham
David Greig
John Guare
Lauren Gunderson
Peter Handke
David Harrower
Jonathan Harvey
Robert Holman
David Ireland
Sarah Kane

Barrie Keeffe
Jasmine Lee-Jones
Anders Lustgarten
Duncan Macmillan
David Mamet
Patrick Marber
Martin McDonagh
Arthur Miller
Alistair McDowall
Tom Murphy
Phyllis Nagy
Anthony Neilson
Peter Nichols
Ben Okri
Joe Orton
Vinay Patel
Joe Penhall
Luigi Pirandello
Stephen Poliakoff
Lucy Prebble
Peter Quilter
Mark Ravenhill
Philip Ridley
Willy Russell
Jackie Sibblies Drury
Sam Shepard
Martin Sherman
Chris Shinn
Wole Soyinka
Simon Stephens
Kae Tempest
Anne Washburn
Laura Wade
Theatre Workshop
Timberlake Wertenbaker
Roy Williams
Snoo Wilson
Frances Ya-Chu Cowhig
Benjamin Zephaniah

For a complete listing of
Methuen Drama titles, visit:

www.bloomsbury.com/drama

Follow us on Twitter and keep up to date
with our news and publications

@MethuenDrama